About
wheels

by JACQUELINE HARDING

Ladybird

Learning Points

This book is designed to introduce young children to the idea of reading.

Learning to read requires many more skills than just decoding words. Children need to learn what a word is, and that reading goes from left to right.

The detailed pictures will give your child clues to what the words say, but most beginning readers will learn the text by heart when the book is repeated several times. This is a normal part of learning to read.

As you go through the book with your child, talk about the pictures and read the text out loud. Move your finger from left to right underneath the words as you say them. One word from the sentence is printed under the picture. Tell your child what the word says and see if he or she can find it in the sentence. Recognizing the shapes of different words is another important part of reading.

If your child is not ready for reading, don't force him or her. Simply enjoy the pictures and the story together.

Acknowledgment
The publishers would like to thank John Dillow
for the cover illustration.

LADYBIRD BOOKS, INC.
Auburn, Maine 04210
Published by LADYBIRD BOOKS LTD.
Loughborough, Leicestershire, U.K.
LADYBIRD and the associated pictorial
device are trademarks of Ladybird Books Ltd.
Printed in Canada

Ladybird Books Inc., Auburn, Maine 04210, U.S.A.
Published by Ladybird Books Ltd., Loughborough, Leicestershire, U.K.

Printed in Canada

About
wheels

by JACQUELINE HARDING
illustrated by GAYNOR CHAPMAN

In the morning the garbage truck came to take the trash.

ONE WAY

garbage truck

The woman missed
the bus.
What will she do?

bus

This truck had to stop
at the side of the road!

truck

The big car towing
the trailer drove
around the truck.

trailer   car

A horse trotted down
the road.
The motorcycle went
past carefully.

motorcycle

The tractor went slowly along the road.

tractor

That car was
going too fast!

car

Beep! Beep!
The taxi was in a
hurry, but there was
too much traffic.

taxi

A pickup truck
broke down in the
middle of the road.

pickup truck

A man helped push the truck to the side of the road so the traffic could get through.

traffic

A man in a tow truck came to help.

tow truck

So much traffic moving slowly ...except

the boy on his bike!